Impressum
Verlag: BABADADA GmbH, Nedderfeld 112 , 22529 Hamburg
Geschäftsführer / Verlagsleitung: Harald Hof
Druck: Books on Demand GmbH, In de Tarpen 42, 22848 Norderstedt

Imprint
Publisher: BABADADA GmbH, Nedderfeld 112 , 22529 Hamburg, Germany
Managing Director / Publishing direction: Harald Hof
Print: Books on Demand GmbH, In de Tarpen 42, 22848 Norderstedt

classroom
교실

divide
나누다

186/2

board
칠판

school yard
학교 운동장

teacher
교사

paper
종이

write
쓰다

pen
펜

desk
책상

ruler
자

book
책

pupil
학생

satchel

책가방

pencil case

필통

pencil

연필

pencil sharpener

연필깎이

rubber

지우개

drawing pad

스케치북

drawing

그림

paintbrush

붓

paint box

그림물감 통

scissors

가위

glue

풀

exercise book

연습장

homework

숙제

number

숫자

add

더하다

subtract

빼다

multiply

곱하다

calculate

계산하다

letter

글자

alphabet

알파벳

word

낱말

text

텍스트

read

읽다

chalk

분필

lesson

수업시간

register

출석부

examination

시험

certificate

증명서

school uniform

교복

education

교육

encyclopedia

백과사전

university

대학교

microscope

현미경

map

지도

waste-paper basket

휴지통

hotel
호텔

hostel
호스텔

currency exchange office
환전소

car
자동차

language
언어

yes / no
예 / 아니오

Okay
좋아

hello
안녕

translator
번역가

Thank you
고마워, 고마워요

how much is...?

... 얼마입니까?

I don't get it

나는 이해하지 못합니다

problem

문제

Good evening!

안녕하세요!

Good morning!

안녕하세요!

Good night!

잘자요!

goodbye

또 만나요

direction

방향

luggage

수하물

bag

가방

backpack

배낭

guest

손님

room

방

sleeping bag

침낭

tent

텐트

tourist information

여행 안내

beach

해변

credit card

신용카드

breakfast

아침식사

lunch

점심식사

dinner

저녁식사

Ticket

승차권

elevator

승강기

stamp

우표

border

경계

customs

세관

embassy

대사관

visa

비자

passport

여권

transport
운반

airplane
비행기

ship
배

fire truck
소방차

truck
화물차

bus
버스

motorboat
모터보트

bike
자전거

car
자동차

ferry

페리

boat

보트

motorbike

오토바이

police car

경찰차

racing car

경주차

rental car

렌트카

car sharing
카셰어링

tow truck
견인차

garbage truck
쓰레기차

engine
모터

fuel
연료

fuel station
주유소

traffic sign
교통 표지

traffic
교통

traffic jam
교통 정체

parking lot
주차장

train station
기차역

tracks
트랙터

train
기차

tram
전차

wagon
객차

helicopter

헬리콥터

airport

공항

tower

타워

passenger

승객

container

컨테이너

carton

상자

cart

카트

basket

바구니

take off / land

출발하다 / 도착하다

city

도시

village

마을

city center

도심

house

집

movie theater 영화관

advert 광고

street light 가로등

street 거리

taxi 택시

snack shop 분식점

pedestrian 보행자

sidewalk 인도

zebra crossing 횡단보도

dumpster 쓰레기통

crossing 교차로

traffic lights 신호등

hut

오두막

apartment

주택

train station

기차역

city hall

시청

museum

박물관

school

학교

university

대학교

bank

은행

hospital

병원

hotel

호텔

pharmacy

약국

office

사무실

book shop

서점

shop

상점

flower shop

꽃가게

supermarket

수퍼마켓

market

시장

department store

백화점

fishmonger's shop

생선가게

mall

쇼핑 센터

harbor

항구

park

공원

bench

벤치

bridge

다리

stairs

계단

subway

지하철

tunnel

터널

bus stop

버스 정류장

bar

바

restaurant

레스토랑

postbox

우체통

street sign

도로 표지판

parking meter

주차료 징수기

zoo

동물원

swimming pool

수영장

mosque

모스크 사원

farm
농장

pollution
환경오염

cemetery
공동묘지

church
교회

playground
놀이터

temple
절

landscape
풍경

signpost
이정표

path
길

meadow
초원

stone
돌

tree
나무

hiker
도보여행자

river
강

grass
잔디

flower
꽃

valley

계곡

hill

산

lake

호수

forest

숲

desert

사막

volcano

화산

castle

성

rainbow

무지개

mushroom

버섯

palm tree

야자나무

mosquito

모기

fly

파리

ant

개미

bee

벌

spider

거미

beetle

딱정벌레

frog

개구리

squirrel

다람쥐

hedgehog

고슴도치

hare

토끼

owl

부엉이

bird

새

swan

백조

boar

맷돼지

deer

사슴

moose

순록

dam

댐

wind turbine

풍력 터빈

solar panel

태양광 전지판

climate

기후

waiter
웨이터

menu
메뉴

chair
의자

soup
수프

pizza
피자

cutlery
수저

tablecloth
테이블보

starter

전채요리

main course

주요리

dessert

후식

drinks

음료수

food

음식

bottle

병

fast food

인스턴트 식품

street food

길거리음식

teapot

찻주전자

sugar bowl

설탕통

portion

인분

espresso machine

에스프레소 머신

high chair

높은 의자

bill

계산서

tray

쟁반

knife

칼

fork

포크

spoon

숟가락

teaspoon

찻숟가락

serviette

냅킨

glass

유리잔

plate

접시

soup plate

수프 그릇

saucer

컵 받침

sauce

소스

salt shaker

소금통

pepper mill

후추통

vinegar

식초

oil

기름

spices

양념

ketchup

케첩

mustard

겨자

mayonnaise

마요네즈

supermarket
수퍼마켓

special offer
특가 판매

customer
고객

dairy products
유제품

fruit
과일

shopping cart
트롤리

butcher's shop

정육점

bakery

빵집

weigh

무게가 나가다

vegetables

채소

meat

고기

frozen food

냉동식품

cold cuts

냉육

canned food

통조림

detergent

가루 세제

candy

달콤한 간식

household products

가정용품

cleaning products

세척제

sales representative

판매원

cash register

계산대

cashier

계산원

shopping list

구매목록

opening hours

문 여는 시간

wallet

지갑

credit card

신용카드

bag

가방

plastic bag

비닐 봉투

water

물

juice

주스

milk

우유

coke

콜라

wine

와인

beer

맥주

alcohol

술

cocoa

카카오

tea

차고

coffee

커피

espresso

에스프레소

cappuccino

카푸치노

banana

바나나

apple

사과

orange

오렌지

melon

수박

lemon

레몬

carrot

당근

garlic

마늘

bamboo

대나무

onion

양파

mushroom

버섯

nuts

견과류

noodles

국수

spaghetti

스파게티

rice

쌀

salad

샐러드

fries

감자칩

fried potatoes

감자튀김

pizza

피자

hamburger

햄버거

sandwich

샌드위치

escalope

커틀렛

ham

햄

salami

살라미

sausage

소시지

chicken

닭

roast

구이

fish

생선

food - 음식

porridge oats

오트밀

muesli

뮤슬리

cornflakes

콘플레이크

flour

밀가루

croissant

크루아상

bread roll

롤빵

bread

빵

toast

토스트

cookies

비스킷

butter

버터

curd

응유

cake

케이크

egg

달걀

fried egg

계란 후라이

cheese

치즈

ice cream

아이스크림

sugar

설탕

honey

꿀

jelly

잼

nougat cream

누가 크림

curry

카레

goat

염소

cow

암소

calf

송아지

pig

돼지

piglet

새끼 돼지

bull

황소

goose
거위

duck
오리

chick
병아리

hen
암탉

cockerel
수탉

rat
쥐

cat
고양이

mouse
생쥐

ox
황소

dog
개

dog house
개집

garden hose
정원용 호스

watering can
물뿌리개

scythe
큰 낫

plow
쟁기

sickle

낫

hoe

괭이

pitchfork

쇠스랑

axe

도끼

pushcart

외바퀴 손수레

trough

여물통

milk can

우유 캔

sack

부대

fence

울타리

stable

축사

greenhouse

비닐하우스

soil

땅

seed

씨앗

fertilizer

거름

combine harvester

콤바인

harvest

수확하다

harvest

수확

yams

참마

wheat

밀

soya

콩

potato

감자

corn

옥수수

rapeseed

유채씨

fruit tree

과일나무

manioc

카사바

grain

곡식

living room

응접실

bathroom

욕실

kitchen

부엌

bedroom

침실

kids room

아이들 방

dining room

식사실

floor

바닥

wall

벽

ceiling

천장

cellar

지하실

sauna

사우나

balcony

발코니

terrace

테라스

pool

수영장

lawn mower

잔디 깎는 기계

sheet

침대 시트

bedspread

이불

bed

침대

broom

빗자루

bucket

양동이

switch

스위치

carpet

카페트

drape

커튼

table

탁자

chair

의자

rocking chair

흔들의자

armchair

안락의자

book

책

blanket

담요

decoration

장식

firewood

뗄감나무

film

영화

stereo system

하이파이 기기

key

열쇠

newspaper

신문

painting

회화

poster

포스터

radio

라디오

notebook

노트

vacuum cleaner

진공청소기

cactus

선인장

candle

초

fridge
냉장고

microwave oven
전자레인지

kitchen scales
주방용 저울

toaster
토스터

laundry detergent
세척제

freezer
냉동실

stove
오븐

dishwasher
식기세제

cooker
쿠커

pot
냄비

cast-iron pot
주철 냄비

wok / kadai
웍 / 카다이 냄비

pan
프라이팬

kettle
주전자

steamer

찜기

baking tray

오븐 구이용 쟁반

crockery

그릇

mug

머그

bowl

양푼이

chopsticks

젓가락

ladle

국자

spatula

주걱

whisk

거품기

strainer

여과기

sieve

체

grater

강판

mortar

절구

barbecue

바베큐

fireplace

화덕

chopping board
도마

rolling pin
밀방망이

corkscrew
코르크 병따개

can
캔

can opener
캔 따개

oven cloth
냄비 받침

sink
개수대

brush
솔

sponge
수세미

blender
블렌더

deep freezer
냉동고

baby bottle
젖병

tap
수도꼭지

shower
샤워

heating
히터

towel
수건

shower curtain
샤워 커튼

bubble bath
거품 비누

bathtub
욕조

glass
유리잔

washing machine
세탁기

tiles
타일

tap
수도꼭지

potty
변기

sink
개수대

toilet
....
화장실

squat toilet
....
재래식 화장실

bidet
....
비데

urinal
....
공중 변소

toilet paper
....
화장지

toilet brush
....
변기솔

toothbrush

칫솔

toothpaste

치약

dental floss

치실

wash

씻다

hand shower

샤워기

douche

질 세척제

basin

대야

back brush

등밀이솔

soap

비누

shower gel

샤워 젤

shampoo

샴푸

flannel

물걸레

drain

배수관

creme

크림

deodorant

체취 제거제

mirror

거울

hand mirror

휴대용 거울

razor

면도기

shaving foam

면도 거품

aftershave

에프터쉐이브

comb

빗

brush

솔

hair-dryer

헤어드라이기

hairspray

헤어스프레이

makeup

메이크업

lipstick

립스틱

nail varnish

손톱깎이

cotton wool

면 솜

nail scissors

손톱

perfume

향수

washbag

세면도구 주머니

stool

스툴

weighing scales

저울

bathrobe

목욕 가운

rubber gloves

고무 장갑

tampon

탐폰

sanitary towel

생리대

chemical toilet

화학 화장실

kids room
아이들 방

alarm clock
자명종

cuddly toy
털인형

toy car
장난감 차

rattle
딸랑이

doll's house
인형의 집

present
선물

balloon
풍선

bed
침대

stroller
유모차

deck of cards
카드 게임

jigsaw
퍼즐

comic
만화

lego bricks
레고

toy blocks
장난감 블럭

action figure
액션 캐릭터

romper suit
베이비 그로

frisbee
프리스비

mobile
모빌

board game
보드 게임

dice
주사위

model train set
기차 모형 세트

pacifier
노리개 젖꼭지

party
파티

picture book
그림책

ball
공

doll
인형

play
놀다

sandpit

모래상자

swing

그네

toys

장난감

video game console

비디오 게임 콘솔

tricycle

세바퀴자전거

teddy bear

곰인형

wardrobe

옷장

clothing

의복

socks

양말

stockings

스타킹

tights

스타킹

scarf
스카프

umbrella
우산

t-shirt
티셔츠

belt
허리띠

boots
부츠

slippers
슬리퍼

sneakers
운동화

sandals

샌들

shoes

신발

rubber boots

고무 장화

underwear

팬티

bra

브래지어

undershirt

러닝 셔츠

clothing - 의복

body

바디

pants

바지

jeans

청바지

skirt

치마

blouse

블라우스

shirt

셔츠

pullover

풀오버

sweater

후드티

blazer

블레이저

jacket

자켓

coat

외투

raincoat

비옷

costume

의상

dress

원피스

wedding dress

웨딩 드레스

suit

양복

nightgown

나이트가운

pajamas

잠옷

sari

사리

headscarf

두건

turban

터번

burka

부르카

kaftan

카프탄

abaya

아바야

swimsuit

수영복

trunks

수영바지

shorts

반바지

tracksuit

트레이닝복

apron

앞치마

gloves

장갑

button

단추

glasses

안경

bracelet

팔찌

necklace

목걸이

ring

반지

earring

귀걸이

cap

캡 모자

coat hanger

옷걸이

hat

모자

tie

넥타이

zip

지퍼

helmet

헬멧

braces

멜빵

school uniform

교복

uniform

유니폼

bib

턱받이

pacifier

노리개 젖꼭지

diaper

기저귀

server
서버

filing cabinet
서류 캐비닛

printer
인쇄기

paper
종이

monitor
모니터

mouse
마우스

desk
책상

folder
폴더

keyboard
자판기

waste-paper basket
휴지통

chair
의자

computer
컴퓨터

coffee mug

커피잔

calculator

계산기

internet

인터넷

laptop

노트북

letter

편지

message

메시지

cell phone

휴대전화

network

네트워크

photocopier

복사기

software

소프트웨어

telephone

전화

plug socket

플러그 소켓

fax machine

팩시밀리

form

서식

document

서류

buy

사다

pay

지불하다

trade

거래하다

money

돈

dollar

달러

euro

유로

yen

엔

rouble

루벨

Swiss franc

스위스 프랑

renminbi yuan

위안

rupee

루피

cash point

현금인출기

currency exchange office

환전소

gold

금

silver

은

oil

석유

energy

에너지

price

가격

contract

계약

tax

세금

stock

주식

work

일하다

employee

근로자

employer

고용주

factory

공장

shop

상점

police officer
경찰관

fireman
소방관

pilot
조종사

doctor
의사

cook
요리사

gardener

정원사

carpenter

목수

seamstress

수선공

judge

판사

chemist

화학자

actor

배우

bus driver

버스운전사

taxi driver

택시 운전사

fisherman

어부

cleaning lady

청소부

roofer

지붕 수리자

waiter

웨이터

hunter

사냥꾼

painter

화가

baker

제빵사

electrician

전기업자

builder

건축업자

engineer

엔지니어

butcher

정육점업자

plumber

배관업자

postman

우편물 배달부

occupations - 직업

soldier

군인

architect

건축가

cashier

계산원

florist

플로리스트

hairdresser

미용사

conductor

검표원

mechanic

정비사

captain

선장

dentist

치과의사

scientist

학자

rabbi

유대교 라비

imam

이맘

monk

수도승

pastor

사제

hammer
망치

screwdriver
나사 드라이버

pliers
펜치

wrench
렌치

torch
손전등

excavator

굴삭기

toolbox

연장통

ladder

사다리

saw

톱

nails

못

drill

드릴

repair
수리하다

shovel
삽

Damn!
젠장!

dustpan
쓰레받기

paint can
페인트통

screws
나사

musical instruments
악기

loud speaker
스피커

drum set
드럼

guitar
기타

double bass
콘트라베이스

trumpet
트럼펫

piano

피아노

violin

바이올린

bass

베이스

timpani

팀파니

drums

북

keyboard

키보드

saxophone

색소폰

flute

플루트

microphone

마이크

tiger
호랑이

entrance
입구

cage
우리

zebra
얼룩말

animal feed
사료

panda
판다 곰

animals

동물

elephant

코끼리

kangaroo

캥거루

rhino

코뿔소

gorilla

고릴라

bear

곰

camel

낙타

ostrich

타조

lion

사자

monkey

원숭이

flamingo

홍학

parrot

앵무새

polar bear

북극곰

penguin

펭귄

shark

상어

peacock

공작

snake

뱀

crocodile

악어

zookeeper

동물원 사육사

seal

물개

jaguar

재규어

pony

조랑말

leopard

표범

hippo

하마

giraffe

기린

eagle

독수리

boar

맷돼지

fish

생선

turtle

거북이

walrus

바다코끼리

fox

여우

gazelle

영양

American football
미식축구

cycling
자전거
경기

tennis
테니스

basketball
농구

swimming
수영

boxing
권투

ice hockey
아이스하키

soccer
축구

badminton
배드민턴

athletics
육상 경기

handball
핸드볼

skiing
스키

polo
폴로

jump
뛰어오르
다

hug
포옹하
다

laugh
웃다

walk
걷다

sing
노래하
다

dream
꿈꾸다

pray
기도하
다

kiss
입맞추
다

write
쓰다

draw
그리다

show
보여주다

push
밀다

give
주다

take
받다

have

가지다

do

행하다

be

...이다

stand

서있다

run

뛰다

pull

당기다

throw

던지다

fall

떨어지다

lie

누워있다

wait

기다리다

carry

운반하다

sit

앉다

get dressed

옷을 입다

sleep

자다

wake up

깨다

look at

보다

cry

울다

stroke

쓰다듬다

comb

빗다

talk

말하다

understand

이해하다

ask

묻다

listen

듣다

drink

마시다

eat

먹다

tidy up

정리하다

love

사랑하다

cook

요리하다

drive

주행하다

fly

날다

sail

해항하다

calculate

계산하다

read

읽다

learn

배우다

work

일하다

marry

결혼하다

sew

바느질하다

brush teeth

이를 닦다

kill

죽이다

smoke

담배 피우다

send

보내다

grandmother
할머니

grandfather
할아버지

father
아버지

mother
어머니

baby
아기

daughter
딸

son
아들

guest

손님

aunt

이모 / 고모

uncle

삼촌

brother

형제

sister

자매

body
몸통

forehead
이마

eye
눈

shoulder
어깨

finger
손가락

face
얼굴

chin
턱

hand
손가락

breast
가슴

leg
다리

arm
팔

baby

아기

man

남자

woman

여자

girl

소녀

boy

소년

head

머리카락

back

등

belly

배

navel

배꼽

toe

발가락

heel

발꿈치

bone

뼈

hip

엉덩이

knee

무릎

elbow

팔꿈치

nose

코

buttocks

둔부

skin

피부

cheek

뺨

ear

귀

lip

입술

mouth

입

tooth

치아

tongue

혀

brain

뇌

heart

심장

muscle

근육

lung

허파

liver

간

stomach

위

kidneys

신장

sex

성교

condom

콘돔

ovum

난자

semen

정자

pregnancy

임신

menstruation

월경

vagina

질

penis

음경

eyebrow

눈썹

hair

머리카락

neck

목

hospital
병원

ambulance
구급차

wheelchair
휠체어

fracture
골절

doctor

의사

emergency room

응급실

nurse

간호사

emergency

응급상황

unconscious

혼수상태

pain

통증

injury

부상

bleeding

출혈

heart attack

심장마비

stroke

뇌졸중

allergy

알러지

cough

기침

fever

열

flu

독감

diarrhea

설사

headache

두통

cancer

암

diabetes

당뇨병

surgeon

외과의

scalpel

수술용 메스

operation

수술

CT

CT

x-ray

엑스레이

ultrasound

초음파

face mask

마스크

disease

질병

waiting room

대기실

crutch

목발

plaster

반창고

bandage

봉대

injection

주사

stethoscope

청진기

stretcher

들것

clinical thermometer

체온계

birth

출생

overweight

과체중

hospital - 병원

hearing aid
보청기

disinfectant
소독약

infection
감염

virus
바이러스

HIV / AIDS
HIV / AIDS

medicine
의학

vaccination
예방접종

tablets
알약

pill
알약

emergency call
구급 전화

blood pressure monitor
혈압측정기

ill / healthy
병든 / 건강한

Help!

도와주세요!

alarm

경보음

assault

폭행

attack

공격

danger

위험

emergency exit

비상구

Fire!

불이야!

fire extinguisher

소화기

accident

사고

first-aid kit

구급 상자

SOS

SOS

police

경찰

Europe

유럽

North America

북미

South America

남미

Africa

아프리카

Asia

아시아

Australia

호주

Atlantic

북극

Pacific

태평양

Indian Ocean

인도양

Antarctic Ocean

남극해

Arctic Ocean

북극해

North pole

북극해

South pole

남극해

Antarctica

남극

earth

지구

land

육지

sea

바다

island

섬

nation

국가

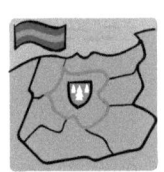

state

주

earth - 지구

clock face

시계 문자판

hour hand

시침

minute hand

분침

second hand

초침

What time is it?

몇 시입니까?

day

일

time

시간

now

지금

digital watch

디지털 시계

minute

분

hour

시간

Monday
월요일

Wednesday
수요일

Friday
금요일

Tuesday
화요일

Saturday
토요일

Thursday
목요일

Sunday
일요일

yesterday
어제

today
오늘

tomorrow
내일

morning
아침

noon
정오

evening
저녁

workdays
근로일

weekend
주말

rain
비

spring
봄

summer
여름

wind
바람

fall
가을

snow
눈

winter
겨울

weather forecast

날씨 예보

thermometer

온도계

sunshine

햇빛

cloud

구름

fog

안개

humidity

습도

lightning

번개

thunder

천둥

storm

폭풍

hail

우박

monsoon

장마

flood

홍수

ice

얼음

January

1월

February

2월

March

3월

April

4월

May

5월

June

6월

July

7월

August

8월

September

9월

October

10월

November

11월

December

12월

shapes
형태

circle

원

square

정사각형

rectangle

직사각형

triangle

삼각형

sphere

구

cube

정사면체

colors
색

white

하양

yellow

노랑

orange

주황

pink

분홍

red

빨강

purple

보라

blue

파랑

green

초록

brown

갈색

gray

회색

black

검정

a lot / a little

많은 / 적은

angry / calm

화난 / 차분한

beautiful / ugly

아름다운 / 추한

beginning / end

시작 / 끝

big / small

큰 / 작은

bright / dark

밝은 / 어두운

brother / sister

형제 / 자매

clean / dirty

깨끗한 / 더러운

complete / incomplete

완전한 / 불완전한

day / night

낮 / 밤

dead / alive

죽은 / 산

wide / narrow

넓은 / 좁은

edible / inedible

삭용의 / 비식용의

evil / kind

불친절한 / 친절한

excited / bored

흥분된 / 지루한

fat / thin

뚱뚱한 / 마른

first / last

처음으로 / 마지막으로

friend / enemy

친구 / 적

full / empty

꽉 찬 / 텅 빈

hard / soft

딱딱한 / 부드러운

heavy / light

무거운 / 가벼운

hunger / thirst

배고픔 / 목마름

ill / healthy

병든 / 건강한

illegal / legal

불법 / 합법

intelligent / stupid

영리한 / 어리석은

left / right

왼 / 오른

near / far

가까운 / 먼

new / used

새 / 헌

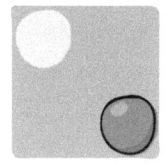

nothing / something

무 / 유

old / young

늙은 / 젊은

on / off

온 / 오프

open / closed

열린 / 닫힌

quiet / loud

조용한 / 시끄러운

rich / poor

부유한 / 가난한

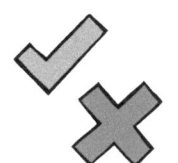

right / wrong

옳은 / 틀린

rough / smooth

거친 / 매끄러운

sad / happy

슬픈 / 기쁜

short / long

짧은 / 긴

slow / fast

느린 / 빠른

wet / dry

젖은 / 마른

warm / cool

따뜻한 / 시원한

war / peace

전쟁 / 평화

0	**1**	**2**
zero	one	two
영	하나	둘
3	**4**	**5**
three	four	five
셋	넷	다섯
6	**7**	**8**
six	seven	eight
여섯	일곱	여덟
9	**10**	**11**
nine	ten	eleven
아홉	열	열하나

12

twelve

열둘

13

thirteen

열셋

14

fourteen

열넷

15

fifteen

열다섯

16

sixteen

열여섯

17

seventeen

열일곱

18

eighteen

열여덟

19

nineteen

열아홉

20

twenty

스물

100

hundred

백

1.000

thousand

천

1.000.000

million

백만

English

영어

American English

미국식 영어

Chinese Mandarin

중국어 만다린

Hindi

힌두어

Spanish

스페인어

French

프랑스어

Arabic

아랍어

Russian

러시아어

Portuguese

포르투갈어

Bengali

불가리아어

German

독일어

Japanese

일본어

I

나

you

너

he / she / it

그 / 그녀/ 그것

we

우리

you

너희들

they

그들

who?

누가?

what?

무엇이?

how?

어떻게?

where?

어디서?

when?

언제?

name

이름

behind

뒤에

in

안에

in front of

앞에

over

위에

on

위에

under

아래에

beside

옆에

between

사이에

place

장소